APRIL

S	M	T	W	T	F	S
		1	2	3	4	5
6	7	8	9	10	11	12
13	14	15	16	17	18	19
20	21	22	23	24	25	26
27	28	29	30			

MAY

S	M	T	W	T	F	S
				1	2	3
4	5	6	7	8	9	10
11	12	13	14	15	16	17
18	19	20	21	22	23	24
25	26	27	28	29	30	31

JUNE

S	M	T	W	T	F	S
1	2	3	4	5	6	7
8	9	10	11	12	13	14
15	16	17	18	19	20	21
22	23	24	25	26	27	28
29	30					

CONTENTS

Best wishes for 2003 Aunty Margaret
Love from
Lesley & Steven xxxx

The
Fireside Book

A picture and a poem
for every mood
chosen by

David Hope

Printed and published by
D.C. THOMSON & CO., LTD.,
185 Fleet Street, LONDON EC4A 2HS.
© D.C. Thomson & Co., Ltd., 2002.
ISBN 0-85116-819-1

CRANHAM WOOD

THIS is the place
That but two weeks ago
Was cocooned in Winter sleep,
Nothing stirred — nothing dared
Disturb the frozen dreams
Of the song thrush
Longing to build
A mud hut
In the hawthorn hedge.

Now on this day
Of heavenly March
The red dead-nettles
Burst into flame
And in the gorse bushes
And cypress trees
The long-tailed tits
Build cathedrals
To give thanks.

David Elder

THE SHEPHERD

HOW sweet is the shepherd's sweet lot!
From the morn to the evening he strays;
He shall follow his sheep all the day,
And his tongue shall be filled with praise.

For he hears the lambs' innocent call,
And he hears the ewes' tender reply:
He is watchful while they are in peace,
For they know when their shepherd is nigh.

William Blake

ENGLISH OAK

FOR the last three hundred years
It's grown erect and tall,
With branches spread like outstretched arms
Protective over all.
Throughout that time it's faced the storms
The snow, the frost and cold,
Undaunted by the elements
It's stood there brave and bold.

As sunshine filters through its leaves
The shadows interplay
Creating dappled light and shade
As branches bend and sway.
And birds come nesting in its boughs
They seem to come and go,
While squirrels with agility
Frisk nimbly to and fro.

And through the seasons of the year
It's changed its leafy dress,
From Springtime green and Autumn tints
To Winter icyness.
And all that time it has endured
And stood there silently,
What is the secret of its strength —
This ancient sturdy tree.

Kathleen Gillum

SEA ROVER

GIVE me the smell of resin and rope,
The sound of the wind at night,
I love the whispering, moonlit waves
The thrill of the early light.
I'm as restless as the changing tide,
Ebbing and filling the bay,
And my heart and soul are stirred again
As I long to sail away.

I've worked in docks and I've farmed the land,
And I've travelled very far,
But I never found a place to rest
Except where the tall ships are.
Give me a star, the creak of the sails,
The waiting time is over,
I gave her my heart and she holds it fast,
The sea — and the old sea rover!

Iris Hesselden

TO MY CAT

THIS look of censure,
  This supercilious stare —
What have I done to incur displeasure?
Did I dare

To tip you out of the comfy seat
When a visitor arrived?
After all, what else could I do?
Don't look so deprived!

Do take that look off your face.
I know I'm in the wrong.
Now you can have your chair back —
She didn't stay too long.

Please forgive me, little one,
My prince of guile and charm.
Hurry then! Jump up again!
The cushion's still quite warm!

Katherine S. White

FOUR-YEAR-OLD

"**S**AY a poem to me," said Clare,
   Lithe-limbed and rosy-cheeked,
Herself a poem.

"Tell me a story, please!"
Her questing ways a tale
With vistas infinite.

"Paint me a picture, now . . ."
Rocking in ready arms
Cessie, her dusky cat;
She stands in her yellow dress —
The picture of joy herself,
Fair, blue-eyed, exquisite.

May C. Jenkins

THE SWIFT

AT daybreak I awoke to find
  A swift had flown into my room —
Errant along the paths of wind
Into the prisoned gloom.
And I arose to set it free,
This wild, quivering bird,
That lay, fear-spent, against my knee,
And yet it neither screamed nor stirred,
But nestled in my hand a space,
And let its long, black wings unbrace,
One moment only — then was gone
Into the white expanse of dawn.

Lawrence Wilson

MEMORY

MY mind lets go a thousand things,
Like dates of wars and deaths of kings,
And yet recalls the very hour —
'Twas noon by yonder village tower,
And on the last blue noon in May —
The wind came briskly up this way,
Crisping the brook beside the road;
Then, pausing here, set down its load
Of pine-scents, and shook listlessly
Two petals from that wild-rose tree.

Thomas Bailey Aldrich

THE LAST DAY OF MAY

ALL day it rained, the river drifting east like mist,
   The town huddled into shrouds.
At eight suddenly before it darkened,
A breach came in the cloud, a deep rift,
Long as a continent, and behind, the swimming of blue.

We went out cautiously, walked to the water,
And by now the whole sky was clearing
As if with panes of stained glass to make a ceiling,
And the moon stood out white
As the pale round of a barn owl's face.

In that light, moths came furring over the river,
Soft things pale as pollen,
Rising in thick clouds through moonlight,
The swallows ticking and flitting among them,
Like millions of scissors.

Kenneth C. Steven

THE SUN-LIT HOUR

CLOSE to the windswept rocks, to watch
The new day now unfold,
Familiar pattern of the skies
In hues of rose and gold,
Reflected in the tranquil sea,
Whose soft lap-lapping tide,
Embosses sand with creamy foam
In circles ever wide;
They trace a course, as old as time's
Eternal ebb and flow,
The surging power of the sea,
With sun-tipped waves aglow.
This special hour of early morn
Whose fresh delightful air,
Now mingles with the sunbeam's rays
For everyone to share!

Elizabeth Gozney

THE TAPESTRY

SOFT green leaves and butterflies
  Birds with tinted wings,
Flowers with velvet faces
A missel-thrush that sings.
Furry fledglings in the nest
The primrose in the lane,
Gossamer of spider webs
Upon the window pane.

Poppies in a field of corn
The hum of fluffy bees,
The glint and gleam of glow-worms
Hiding 'neath the trees.
Nature works with unseen hand
With artistry and skill
Upon the tapestry of life
Her purpose to fulfil.

Kathleen Gillum

DAY TRIP

AN eager band of travellers,
The winding way to wend,
A show, of yellow sunbeams,
On wistful wings transcends.

A colour chart delights the eye,
Of floribunda fair,
The picket fences, white and spruce,
Quaint churches filled with prayer.

To saunter on the promenade,
Gipsy fortune's spell, to yield,
A light mist, from the ocean's fret,
Crabs and shrimps appeal.

A cargo light, of laughter lends
This carefree company,
A rendezvous of happy hours,
Beside a sapphire sea.

Dorothy McGregor

THE SPIRIT OF SUMMER

I AM the song Midsummer sings;
The harvest of the grain.
I am full moon that golden swings;
The wind that brings the rain.

I am the swallow in the sky;
The little drifting cloud.
I am the bright-winged butterfly;
The sunflower standing proud.

I am the yew tree, dark and old;
The hawk above the grass.
I am a tale the shepherd told
The farmer's blue-eyed lass.

I am the hill that stands alone;
The sunset's gaudy gleams.
I am all Summers you have known
And treasure in your dreams.

Peter Cliffe

GOLDFINCH

ONLY a doge or Tuscan duke
Could get away with those colours —
Black and red and gold.
As for a portrait
By Piero della Francesca or Boticelli
You pose on the teasel throne,
And beneath the hazy blue
Beatific sky
Merge with the Summer fresco.

David Elder

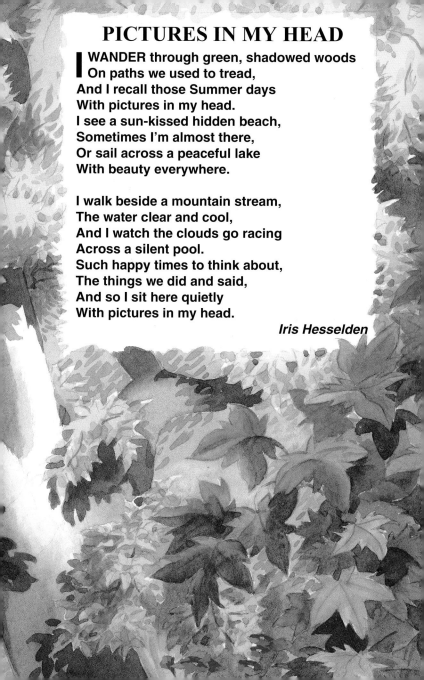

PICTURES IN MY HEAD

I WANDER through green, shadowed woods
On paths we used to tread,
And I recall those Summer days
With pictures in my head.
I see a sun-kissed hidden beach,
Sometimes I'm almost there,
Or sail across a peaceful lake
With beauty everywhere.

I walk beside a mountain stream,
The water clear and cool,
And I watch the clouds go racing
Across a silent pool.
Such happy times to think about,
The things we did and said,
And so I sit here quietly
With pictures in my head.

Iris Hesselden

FALSE PROPHET

THE weatherman's dead hopeless;
He really is a twit.
He promises a heatwave.
And what we get ain't it!

The weatherman's quite useless;
I'd love to tell him that.
He said we'd have a dry spell,
And a cloudburst drowned the cat.

He claims to be an expert,
But I think he's a goof.
He said we'd have a gentle breeze,
So what blew off the roof?

Satellites and weather ships
To help the chap along;
So why is it, I wonder,
He ALWAYS gets it wrong?

Peter Cliffe

THE WELL

I FOUND a well once
In the dark green heart of a wood
Where pigeons ruffled up into a skylight of branches
And disappeared.

The well was old, so mossed and broken
It was almost a part of the wood

Gone back to nature. Carefully, almost fearfully,
I looked down into its depths

And saw the lip of water shifting and tilting
Heard the music of dripping stones.

I stretched down, cupped a deep handful
Out of the Winter darkness of its world

And drank. That water tasted of moss, of secrets,
Of ancient meetings, of laughter,

Of dark stone, of crystal —
It reached the roots of my being

Assuaged a whole Summer of thirst.
I have been wandering for that water ever since.

Kenneth C. Steven

FAIRIES

SHOULD you walk in woods of pine
Some scented evening, you may find
That you can hear the tinkling sound
Of fairy laughter all around.
Those little creatures love to tease
They hide themselves behind the trees.

But you may see them in disguise,
Pretending to be butterflies
When, high against the evening sky,
Those fairies of the forest fly
With rainbows in their silver wings,
And promises of magic things.

Katherine S. White

MIDSUMMER JOURNEY

DEEP-shadowed woods, green to the heart's core,
    Wearing mid-Summer like a garment strewn
With pallid wind-flowers, trails of briar rose
And willow-lace spun from the webs of June.
Birch filigrees, syringa's clustered stars,
Roses in bright profusion boldly tossed
On ghost-grey walls and velvet textured lawns
Scattered with golden-centred daisy frost.
Elms in their sweeping gowns, broad chestnut boughs
Casting exotic shade on haunted grass.
Swift rush of shining beech leaves briefly seen
And river-glimpses gleaming as we pass.

Joan Howes

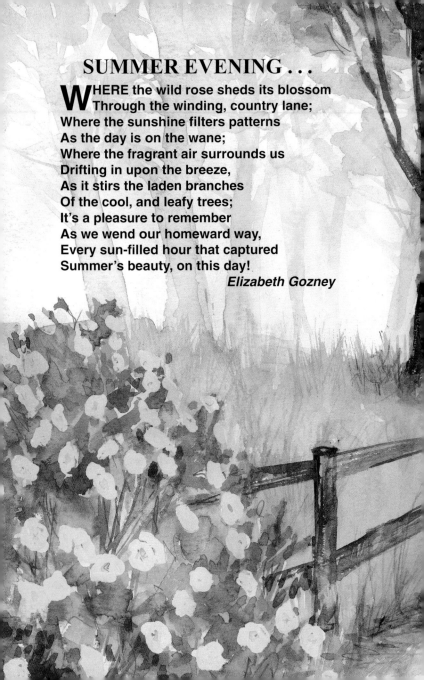

SUMMER EVENING . . .

WHERE the wild rose sheds its blossom
Through the winding, country lane;
Where the sunshine filters patterns
As the day is on the wane;
Where the fragrant air surrounds us
Drifting in upon the breeze,
As it stirs the laden branches
Of the cool, and leafy trees;
It's a pleasure to remember
As we wend our homeward way,
Every sun-filled hour that captured
Summer's beauty, on this day!

Elizabeth Gozney

SWALLOWS, RIVER DEE

LIKE ballerinas — elegant and sleek,
Confident of their next move
They dance and pirouette
To the music in the sky.

And when the curtain falls
They curtsey on the Dee
To drink a toast
To Summer.

David Elder

THE MUSIC OF
THE NIGHT

LISTEN to the music,
　The voices of the night:
The wind that gently rustles
Like angel wings in flight.
The murmur of the ocean
Across the silent shore,
Caressing sand and pebbles,
She sings forever more.

The distant drone of aircraft
On some exotic flight,
The far-off hum of traffic,
Still moving through the night.
A steeple clock keeps chiming,
Swift footsteps running by,
And then the rain falls softly,
A soothing lullaby.

Before the sun awakens
To fill the world with light,
Just listen to the voices,
The music of the night.

Iris Hesselden

THE TRANQUIL HOUR . . .

WE all need time to stand and stare
 By river's still and tranquil air;
To stroll through leafy wood's retreat,
In welcome shade, from Summer's heat!
And later, see a rainbow etch,
A pastel arc — a painter's sketch;
A vista where we play a part
To share the joys of nature's art,
Whose sunset's image through the trees,
Brings perfect moments, such as these . . .
. . . We all need time to stand and stare,
To view life's beauty — everywhere . . .

Elizabeth Gozney

SOLSTICE NIGHT CLIMB

FAR below, Fort William glitters
  In a treasure-trove of lights
Guarded by the Nevis dragon.

The Ben hunches down,
Tail of path swishing through the dusk,
Back and forth,
In age-old patience.

From glens' nostrils come puffs of cloud;
Lichen scales and sharp teeth of scree
Gleam in moonlight;
One baleful eye blinks as a map is checked.

Summer solstice casts its spell,
Even industry now a fairy castle,
Its blazing ramparts reflecting in Loch Eil's moat.

Rowena M. Love

BANISHED IS SLEEP

THE tissues of dawn
Dissolve in the dew.
Golden sun-shafts split
The fragile sky wide open,
And diva-like songbirds
Lead the chorus of day.
Sheep, recently sheared, bleat
To another morning greet,
While silken-winged butterflies
Gaily flutter through the air.
With fishes in their throats,
Silver streams gurgle towards
The gaping mouth of the sea.
Weeping willows droop wearily,
As in lush grass-green meads
Timid creatures emerge to peep.
Banished is sleep.

Glynfab John

PATCHWORK PIECES

PATCHWORK pieces, fingers flying,
  Grandma talking as she sews,
Me beside her, knee-high, listening,
Watching as her quilting grows.
Every piece contains a story,
Every fabric tells its tale,
This one speaks of distant dance days,
That one whispers wedding veil.
"Here's some blue from baby's rompers,
White from Grandad's Sunday shirt,
Stripes from Bobby's best pyjamas,
Polka-dots from Katy's skirt."
Patterns grow in rainbow pieces,
"Can you guess? Oh, yes, it's true —
Yellow from your mummy's sundress
When she was as small as you."
Now those quilting days are over,
Yet the stitches still hold fast,
Now I sleep 'neath Grandma's patchwork
Loved as long as memories last.

Margaret Ingall

MEETING AT NIGHT

THE gray sea and the long black land;
  And the yellow half-moon large and low;
And the startled little waves that leap
In fiery ringlets from their sleep,
As I gain the cove with pushing prow,
And quench its speed i' the slushy sand.

Then a mile of warm sea-scented beach;
Three fields to cross till a farm appears;
A tap at the pane, the quick sharp scratch
And blue spurt of a lighted match,
And a voice less loud, thro' its joys and fears,
Than the two hearts beating each to each!

Robert Browning

RACING FOR HOME

ENTERING the final strait,
Seacat races for Troon
white horses galloping in her wake.
Mounted with rainbows by the setting sun,
their flamboyant silks flutter in the breeze.

A passing yacht tic-tacs the odds
as guillemots,
hoarse as hardened racegoers,
shout home the favourite.

Fishing boats jockey for position,
fighting for a place;
like shredded betting slips
scavengers swirl above them,
gambling on the toss of heads or tails.

Rowena M. Love

SHOES

THE shoemaker stitched and sewed
 In the dark scent of his own world. Once a year
I went in there, to the black adverts for boots and polish
Rusty over the walls of his shop. I blinked

Like something that had tumbled down a hole
Into the heart of the earth. Even the air was tanned,
The chestnut of shoes burnished and perfect from hands
That had poured in the pure oils of their love,

Their labour. He wiped those huge hands on his apron
Stood as I smoothed my feet into the mended shoes,
Looking, his eyes like a calf's, brown
In an air that was brown, a brown cave.

The scent of leather hung in the air
In my shoes that were good as new,
That fitted my feet like hooves —
They shone so I saw my own smile.

I went out into the blue breeze of the Springtime
Watching my step, all the way home. Still,
School scuffed them and skinned them,
Reduced them at last to a shadow of all they had been.

Kenneth C. Steven

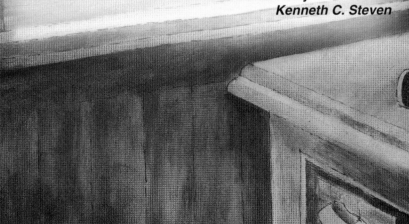

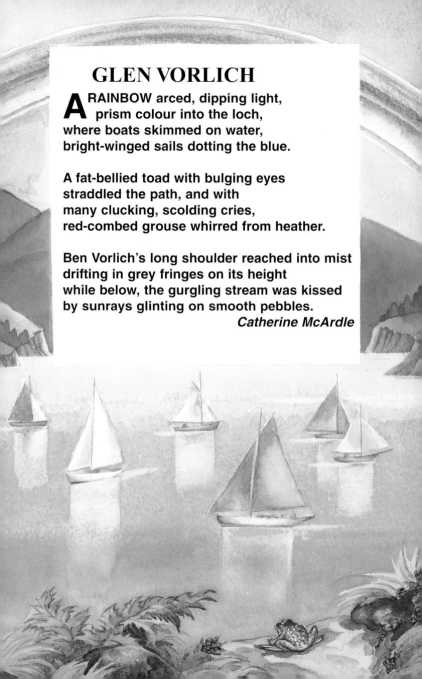

GLEN VORLICH

A RAINBOW arced, dipping light,
  prism colour into the loch,
where boats skimmed on water,
bright-winged sails dotting the blue.

A fat-bellied toad with bulging eyes
straddled the path, and with
many clucking, scolding cries,
red-combed grouse whirred from heather.

Ben Vorlich's long shoulder reached into mist
drifting in grey fringes on its height
while below, the gurgling stream was kissed
by sunrays glinting on smooth pebbles.

Catherine McArdle

SKYSCAPE

AS sunshine streams across the sky
Upon this windless day,
Feathery clouds like sailing ships
Glide slowly on their way.
Frothy billows in the blue
In silence move and fade,
Forming castles in the air
Which change with light and shade.

These alabaster images
Artistic in design,
Interspersed with pastel tints
Seem delicate and fine.
Contrasting the white-fringed clouds
Are many birds in flight,
Climbing, swooping, plummeting
Beyond the range of sight.

They dip and dive and wheel and weave
Forever flying free,
Acrobatics in the air —
Soaring gracefully.
These tiny forms in silhouette
Specks to the naked eye,
Have made their playground up among
The sculptures in the sky.

Kathleen Gillum

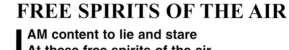

FREE SPIRITS OF THE AIR

I AM content to lie and stare
At these free spirits of the air,
The loved sandmartins that have come
To scrape their cunning tunnelled home
In this now-wasted sandy bluff
I hope is soft and tall enough:
To see the good-luck swallow sail
With turning wing and fork-shaped tail,
And highest in the sparkling light
The swifts like boomerangs in flight,
While gliding seagulls I can spy,
Free spirits of the boundless sky.

Glynfab John

CATS

THE cat flowed round the open door
Like a wavelet on a stream,
Casts eyes right and left, checking
For its extinct predators.
The cat paw-stepped silently
(Like a child trying tiptoes)
Over to the bulky armchair
Where the woman sat snoring.
The flickering lights, unobserved,
Showed taut African grasslands
And lions mauling their dead prey
Under certain, casual skies.
The cat sprung on to her lap,
Purred, kneaded the soft thighs
And curled up, happy, for an hour
To forget being a cat.

Hamish Brown

THE HAZELNUT WOOD

THE world had turned on its axis,
   Lay a little into the west wind,
So the shoulders of the hills were visited
With a silking of snow.

My mother took me to the nut wood
On a day blue as an eggshell;
The streams went by like trinkets, jewellery,
Shining with September's rains.

They were dry and shiny things,
Fat and russet in their coverings,
Falling when wind lifted the treetops
In dark thuds at our feet.

The white insides were sweet,
Split on the teeth and filled the mouth,
The mind, with all the ripeness
Of a long Summer sun.

Kenneth C. Steven

CLOSE-UP
IN GLEN AFFRIC

TO the discreet percussion
Of falling water, where pines
Grow out of rock-faces, we dined:

As if she'd been expecting us,
A chaffinch landed on our table and
Solicited first bite of Beauly bread.

Her mate, arriving seconds later,
Was not so subtle, bounced
Around in his royal colours,

Hopped bravely up and skewered
His share from right between
Extended forefinger and thumb,

Then shot off to a twig
For a secret helping before
Returning to parental duty:

Once recovered from the shock,
We played at statues
Till the encore could be photographed.
Ian Nimmo White

CIRCLE

SLOW down the seasons, they're turning too fast!
Spring is delightful, but quickly slips past,
Summer is beautiful, peaches and cream,
Long days and holidays pass like a dream.
Autumn comes swiftly, with russet and red,
A glorious canopy over my head,
Winter comes creeping soon, misty and chill,
Lights in the city and snow on the hill.
The circle keeps spinning, the year rushing past,
Slow down the seasons, they're turning too fast!

Iris Hesselden

SEEING

THERE will be only a few days like this —
The low sun flinting the house
Through the green sea of the trees as you stand
Struck, blessed, bathed in the same light
That rose life once from the young earth, that appled
The first child's cheeks.
There will be only a few days like this
To stop doing and stand, blinking,
As the leverets tumble in the bright field
And a cuckoo's moss voice calls from a far wood.
Wait until the sun has gone in broken orange
Down beneath the hills, and the blue sky
Hurts with the sudden shudder of the dusk.
Give thanks and turn and go back home —
For there will be only a few days like this.

Kenneth C. Steven

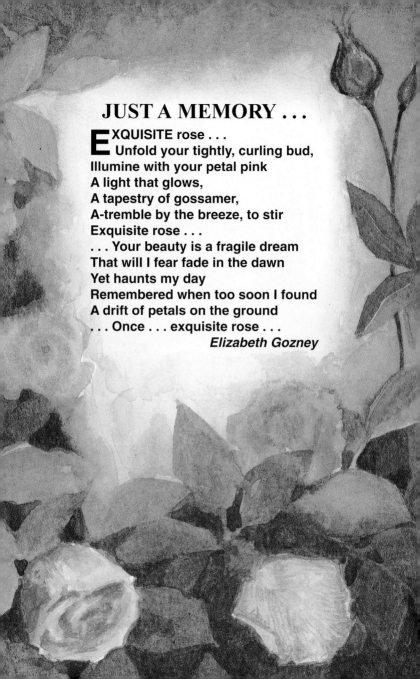

JUST A MEMORY . . .

EXQUISITE rose . . .
Unfold your tightly, curling bud,
Illumine with your petal pink
A light that glows,
A tapestry of gossamer,
A-tremble by the breeze, to stir
Exquisite rose . . .
. . . Your beauty is a fragile dream
That will I fear fade in the dawn
Yet haunts my day
Remembered when too soon I found
A drift of petals on the ground
. . . Once . . . exquisite rose . . .

Elizabeth Gozney

RUSTIC TAPESTRY

LIKE chequered prints the Autumn tints
Are splashed across the land,
A coloured canvas deftly wrought
By nature's skilful hand.
A patchwork quilt of many shades
Some subtle, others bold,
It seems the countryside is clothed
In garments dipped in gold.

And from the trees the trembling leaves
Are gently drifting down,
Crimson, amber, bronze and red
And yellow turning brown.
Gliding slowly to the earth
They fall without a sound,
And find at last a resting place
Carpeting the ground.

Fields and woods and fertile soil
All blend in harmony,
Against the backdrop of the hills —
A rustic tapestry.
To those who have observant eyes
And ponder nature's ways,
There's satisfying beauty in
These mellow Autumn days.

Kathleen Gillum

CONKERS

IN those Autumns of childhood
  That have cartwheeled away through the woods
   like jesters,

In the undergrowth of my memory
I find the thrill of going for conkers

On tousled mornings when the leaves rampaged
Across the fields and trees were bent

Like tired warriors. I ran and ran
As sudden sunlight scattered in a dust of gold

And shocked the dark October woods
With warmth like smiling.

I found them. Lacquered mahogany things
That smelled of all the living brownness of the earth,

The richest loam of Autumn
The secrecy of Hallowe'en.

Kenneth C. Steven

THE EAGLE

HE clasps the crag with crooked hands;
  Close to the sun in lonely lands,
Ring'd with the azure world he stands.

The wrinkled sea beneath him crawls;
He watches from his mountain walls,
And like a thunderbolt he falls.

Lord Tennyson

FULL MOON

THE clear night
scatters stars across
a wide firmament
gilded with sparks.

In the tranquil
stillness a whole moon
hangs like a cheese
blessing the earth.

The sharp frost
has driven all
manner of creatures
indoors, even the cat.

The moon swims
in a starry soup,
shining brightly
above, heaven's light.

Peter Cardwell

WINTER'S HERE

A STARK white Winter wonderland
Is awesome nature's shift.
Embraced in all its purity
To set our hearts adrift.

Bleached the sheet on which to write,
A crisp and bright new morn,
Swift the sleigh on silver ice,
Sweet memories are born.

Is Winter's shawl around us
A frozen, naked breath,
So stunning is the landscape
A renewal of our faith.

Dorothy McGregor

LANDING AT ABBOTSINCH

ON the slow descent,
   dykes gouge the snow-barked fields,
carving as deeply as lovers' initials
in an ancient tree.
Then neon spores speckle city below
like lichen on the trunk of night;
wrapping round that dear green place,
the mistletoe of Clyde,
druid-dark where it absorbs the light.

Rowena M. Love

RIGID MIDNIGHT

WATCHING the water flow
on a freezing night like this,
so cold
you can almost see molecules
slow and slow and become
glued to the cracking banks.
Below the glistening bridge,

nothing seems to stir
on either side.
The world seems stuck
while the ice sucks silver
motion, slowly
from the river,
and stills it in the glittering midnight.

Shimmering, the river sludges to a grudging halt.
Above, Orion looks out crystal
from his sloping perch among the stars,
hunting the horizon,
while frost grips the ground
turning trees into
sparkling melodramas.

Adam Johnson

WORLD OF WHITE

BEAUTIFUL world of white on white
When snowflakes start to fall,
And nature tiptoes silently
To spread her fleecy shawl.
The icy feathers flutter down
And drift through time and space,
Covering all the countryside
With wisps of dainty lace.

It seems a fairy visitor
Has danced across the land,
Scattering her silver dust
Dispensed by frozen hand.
On tinselled twigs and frozen boughs
The frosted gems appear,
And crystal shapes and icicles
Are glistening bright and clear.

The chimney pots and village school
The church of weathered stone,
Transformed by Winter's downy quilt
Add beauty of their own.
The sparkling mantle of the snow
Contrasts the inky night —
The sleeping town awakens to
A dazzling world of white.

Kathleen Gillum

FROSTY MORNING

AS the mercury falls,
silver rises:
land dipped white
engraved with shadows.

Cobwebs are tied to eaves
with marcasite threads,
frost rimming them to snowflakes.

From roofs enamelled black by sunshine
crows look on, like agents,
as robins pose for Christmas card gardens.

Rowena M. Love

CHRISTMAS EVE

WARM and prepared, the house is sleeping now.
Children, at last, have closed reluctant eyes.
Serene as faith, the window candles burn,
Piercing the night with radiant mysteries.
Snow blurs the dreaming panes with gauzy breath,
Pressing its cold, white face against the door.
The sound of altar bells has died away,
Leaving an aching stillness, where before
Sweet notes of carolling and mingled prayer
Flowed from beneath a slender, ancient spire.
The spell of Christmas gilds the waiting hours —
And reminiscent cows kneel in the byre.

Joan Howes

CHRISTMAS TREAT

THROUGH the Christmas Fair they wander,
 Feasting on each magic sight:
Helter skelters, festive sideshows
All combine for their delight.

"Little brother, here's a penny,
Spend it on the carousel" —
She has saved one coin, to lavish
On the lad she loves so well.

He has never seen a fairground,
Treats are rare for this small boy,
Yet he spends his only penny
On a gift to bring her joy.

"Sister, take these pretty ribbons —
When the shows have gone away,
Wear them and we'll share the magic
Of the fair, on Christmas Day."

Glynfab John